DOGS SET IX

BORDER COLLIES

Joanne Mattern
ABDO Publishing Company

visit us at
www.abdopublishing.com

Published by ABDO Publishing Company, 8000 West 78th Street, Edina, Minnesota 55439. Copyright © 2012 by Abdo Consulting Group, Inc. International copyrights reserved in all countries. No part of this book may be reproduced in any form without written permission from the publisher. The Checkerboard Library™ is a trademark and logo of ABDO Publishing Company.

Printed in the United States of America, North Mankato, Minnesota.
062011
092011

 PRINTED ON RECYCLED PAPER

Cover Photo: Photolibrary
Interior Photos: Alamy pp. 17, 19; Animals Animals p. 11; AP Images p. 9; Corbis p. 7;
    Mark Raycroft / Minden Pictures / National Geographic Stock p. 13;
    Photolibrary pp. 5, 6, 18; Thinkstock pp. 15, 20, 21

Editors: Megan M. Gunderson, BreAnn Rumsch
Art Direction: Neil Klinepier

Library of Congress Cataloging-in-Publication Data

Mattern, Joanne, 1963-
  Border collies / Joanne Mattern.
     p. cm. -- (Dogs)
  Includes index.
  ISBN 978-1-61714-989-4
  1. Border collie--Juvenile literature. I. Title.
  SF429.B64M29 2012
  636.737'4--dc22
                                        2011009033

CONTENTS

THE DOG FAMILY

Dogs and people have been friends for thousands of years. Long ago, dogs became one of the first **domesticated** animals. Humans used them as hunting companions. Later, dogs also herded and guarded other animals.

Scientists believe dogs descended from the gray wolf. Today, there are more than 400 different dog **breeds**. All these dogs come in many shapes and sizes. Yet they are all part of the family **Canidae**. This name comes from the Latin word *canis*, which means "dog."

Several dog breeds are used to herd sheep. One of the most outstanding herding dogs is the Border collie. This dog is a hard worker as well as a loving, loyal pet.

The word collie is a Scottish dialect word that describes sheepdogs.

BORDER COLLIES

Humans have depended on hardworking herding dogs for hundreds of years. In Great Britain, people used many different **breeds** to manage large herds of sheep. The dogs moved the sheep around and kept them from wandering away. They also protected the sheep from predators.

In Scotland, dogs originally called Scotch sheep dogs were popular with shepherds. Some of these dogs lived along the border of Scotland and England. So eventually, they became known as Border collies.

6

Border collies often stare hard at animals they want to herd. This is called "eye." It lets the other animals know who's boss!

In 1860, people began showing Border collies at dog shows. Starting in 1876, people began holding herding contests.

Soon, many people became interested in these intelligent dogs! They brought the dogs to the United States, where they remained important to sheepherders. The **American Kennel Club (AKC)** recognized the Border collie as part of its herding group in 1995.

WHAT THEY'RE LIKE

Border collies are incredibly smart. So, it is important to keep these dogs active. This will help prevent them from getting bored and misbehaving.

These energetic dogs love having a job to do! Border collies with good temperaments may work as **therapy** dogs. Others help police and emergency workers rescue people from disasters.

Border collies are usually friendly. They may be wary of strangers, but they love their families! These athletic dogs enjoy exercising and playing games with their owners. Many people enter their Border collies in **agility** competitions, where the dogs can run and jump.

Pet Border collies can still display the herding instinct. Some will try to herd just about anything that moves. That includes rakes, snow shovels, vacuum cleaners, and even children!

Border collies love competition!

COAT AND COLOR

The Border collie has a thick double coat. The soft inner coat is short, **dense**, and warm. The outer coat is more coarse and either straight or wavy. The double coat resists water and protects the dog from harsh weather.

The Border collie's coat comes in two varieties. The rough coat is medium in length. It features **feathering** on the forelegs, haunches, chest, and underside. The coat is short on the face, ears, feet, and fronts of the legs.

The smooth coat is short all over. It often has a coarser texture than the rough coat. This variety can feature a little feathering on the forelegs, haunches, chest, and neck.

The **AKC** accepts solid color, bicolor, tricolor, **merle**, and **sable** Border collies. Many bicolor Border collies are black and white. Tricolor dogs often feature black, brown, and white. Other coat colors are slate gray, tan, **brindle**, fawn, blue, blue merle, red, red merle, and lilac.

Whether rough or smooth, your dog's coat will shed in early summer as the weather gets warmer.

SIZE

Border collies are medium-sized dogs. They usually weigh between 31 and 50 pounds (14 and 23 kg). Male dogs are a little taller than females. Males measure 19 to 22 inches (48 to 56 cm) tall at the **withers**. Females stand 18 to 21 inches (46 to 53 cm) tall.

A Border collie is slightly longer than it is tall. Its strong **muzzle** tapers slightly to the nose. The tips of its medium-sized ears may flop forward or stand upright.

This **breed**'s eyes are medium sized and oval in shape. They can be brown or blue. Some dogs have one blue eye and one brown eye!

The Border collie breed has an alert, eager expression.

CARE

Border collies need a lot of exercise and attention. **Agility** competitions, fetch, jogging, swimming, and hiking are all great ways to satisfy this **breed**.

Give your Border collie's coat attention, too. Keep the coat healthy by brushing it weekly. Bathe your dog every few weeks or whenever it gets really dirty.

Also, brush you dog's teeth at least several times a week. Carefully clean its ears. And, make sure to clip your pet's nails short.

A Border collie should see a veterinarian at least once a year. The veterinarian will check the dog's general health and give it **vaccines**. He or she can **spay** or **neuter** dogs that are not going to be bred.

Border collies are generally healthy. But, a few serious medical problems can affect some. These dogs may have hearing or vision problems. This **breed** can also suffer from **hip dysplasia** and other joint problems.

Vaccines are a vital part of keeping your dog healthy.

FEEDING

Border collies want to be involved in everything you do. Eating a high-quality food will give them the energy they need. Border collies can eat dry, wet, or semimoist food. A veterinarian can recommend the best food to keep your dog healthy, happy, and strong.

The veterinarian can also tell owners how much to feed their dogs. A puppy should eat three to four small meals a day. Once the dog is at least six months old, it can be fed two larger meals each day.

Border collies need plenty of water to stay healthy. Dogs should always have a clean bowl of fresh water available. The active Border collie will especially need a drink after exercising and during hot weather.

It's best not to feed your dog table scraps. Some people foods are unsafe for dogs, and they can lead to weight gain.

THINGS THEY NEED

Border collies are energetic! They enjoy long periods of exercise and play every day. Owners should provide a safe place where their dogs can run, such as a fenced yard.

Obedience training is important for all **breeds**, especially Border collies. These intelligent dogs need to learn the rules and to obey their owners.

A healthy coat looks glossy but is not too oily.

Training will teach Border collies to follow commands, such as coming when called. And, it will prevent problem behaviors such as chewing, digging, jumping up, and barking too much.

Every Border collie needs certain items to keep it safe. A leash and a collar with license and

Healthy adult dogs can run all day and still have energy to play!

identification tags are a must. A Border collie should also have a crate to rest in, especially when its owners are away.

PUPPIES

Like other dogs, female Border collies are **pregnant** for about 63 days after mating. Medium-sized dog **breeds** usually have four to eight puppies in a **litter**.

Puppies should have several short exercise periods every day.

Border collie puppies cannot see or hear until they are 10 to 14 days old. Their mother takes care of them for about six to eight weeks. Then, the puppies are old enough to go to a new home.

It is important to **socialize** Border collie puppies. Give them lots of new experiences! Puppies should learn to play with other dogs and get used to being around people. This will help them become friendly, loving members of their new families. Healthy Border collies will live about 15 years.

GLOSSARY

agility - a sport in which a handler leads a dog through an obstacle course during a timed race.

American Kennel Club (AKC) - an organization that studies and promotes interest in purebred dogs.

breed - a group of animals sharing the same ancestors and appearance. A breeder is a person who raises animals. Raising animals is often called breeding them.

brindle - having dark streaks or spots on a gray, tan, or tawny background.

Canidae (KAN-uh-dee) - the scientific Latin name for the dog family. Members of this family are called canids. They include wolves, jackals, foxes, coyotes, and domestic dogs.

dense - thick or compact.

domesticated - adapted to life with humans.

feathering - a fringe of hair.

hip dysplasia (HIHP dihs-PLAY-zhuh) - unusual formation of the hip joint.

litter - all of the puppies born at one time to a mother dog.

merle - having dark patches of color on a lighter background.

muzzle - an animal's nose and jaws.

neuter (NOO-tuhr) - to remove a male animal's reproductive glands.

pregnant - having one or more babies growing within the body.

sable - having black-tipped hairs on a silver, gold, gray, fawn, or brown background.

socialize - to accustom an animal or a person to spending time with others.

spay - to remove a female animal's reproductive organs.

therapy - relating to the treatment of diseases and disorders.

vaccine (vak-SEEN) - a shot given to prevent illness or disease.

withers - the highest part of a dog's or other animal's back.

WEB SITES

To learn more about Border collies, visit ABDO Publishing Company online. Web sites about Border collies are featured on our Book Links page. These links are routinely monitored and updated to provide the most current information available.

www.abdopublishing.com

23

INDEX